LET'S-READ-AND-FIND-OUT SCIENCE®

STAGE 1

How a Seed Grows

by Helene J. Jordan • illustrated by Loretta Krupinski

HarperCollinsPublishers

*The illustrations in this book were painted on
three-ply Strathmore Bristol board in gouache with colored pencils.*

The *Let's-Read-and-Find-Out Science* book series was originated by Dr. Franklyn M. Branley, Astronomer Emeritus and former Chairman of the American Museum–Hayden Planetarium, and was formerly co-edited by him and Dr. Roma Gans, Professor Emeritus of Childhood Education, Teachers College, Columbia University. Text and illustrations for each of the books in the series are checked for accuracy by an expert in the relevant field. For more information about Let's-Read-and-Find-Out Science books, write to HarperCollins Children's Books, 10 East 53rd Street, New York, NY 10022, or visit our web site at http://www.harperchildrens.com.

HarperCollins®, ♠®, and Let's Read-and-Find-Out Science® are trademarks of HarperCollins Publishers Inc.

HOW A SEED GROWS
Text copyright © 1960, 1992 by Helene Jordan Waddell
Illustrations copyright © 1992 by Loretta Krupinski

Library of Congress Cataloging-in-Publication Data
Jordan, Helene J. (Helene Jamieson)
   How a seed grows / by Helene J. Jordan ; illustrated by Loretta Krupinski. — Rev. ed.
      p.   cm. — (Let's-read-and-find-out science. Stage 1)
   Summary: Uses observations of bean seeds planted in eggshells to demonstrate the growth of seeds into plants.
   ISBN 0-06-020104-5. — ISBN 0-06-020185-1 (lib. bdg.). — ISBN 0-06-445107-0 (pbk.)
   1. Germination—Juvenile literature.   2. Seeds—Juvenile literature.   [1. Seeds.]   I. Krupinski, Loretta, ill.
II. Title.   III. Series.
QK740.J67   1992
582'.0166—dc20
                                                                                          91-10166
                                                                                          CIP
                                                                                          AC

Revised Edition

A seed is a little plant. It is a plant that has not started to grow. Apple trees and daisies, carrots and corn, clover and wheat, all grow from seeds.

Here is a tree seed.

Someday it will be a tree like this.

Here is a flower seed.

Someday it will be a flower like this.

Some seeds grow slowly. These are the seeds of an oak tree.

An oak tree grows very, very slowly. Suppose you planted an oak tree seed. You would be a father or a mother, or even a grandfather or a grandmother, and the oak tree would still be growing.

Some seeds grow fast. This is a bean seed.

It grows very fast. It grows so fast that it becomes a bean plant in just a few weeks.

You can plant bean seeds yourself. We used pole beans. You can use pole beans, bush beans, or lima beans.

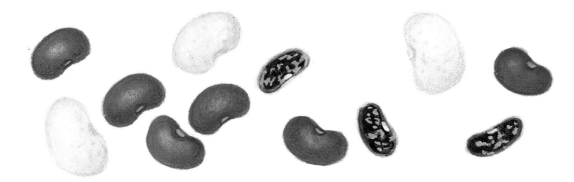

You can plant the seeds in eggshells or tin cans or old cups or little flowerpots. Be sure that your containers have holes in the bottom.

We used eggshells. We used
a pencil to make holes in the
eggshells.

We filled twelve eggshells with
soil like this.

We made a hole in the soil with
a finger, like this.

When you have made a hole in
the soil, plant a bean seed in it.
Plant one seed in each hole.

Cover the seed with soil.

Sprinkle the soil carefully with a little water.

Number the shells. Write the number 1 on the first shell. Put the number 2 on the next shell. Keep going until all of the shells are numbered from 1 to 12.

13

Put all the eggshells in an egg carton.

Put the carton in sunlight on a windowsill.

Some bean seeds grow faster than others. Our seeds began to grow in three days. Your bean seeds may take a little longer.

You won't be able to see your seeds growing yet. They start to grow under the soil where you can't see them.

Water your seeds a little every day.

The water soaks into the seeds. The seeds begin to grow.

More water soaks into the seeds. The seeds get fatter and fatter.

17

Wait for three days and then dig up seed Number 1.

It may be soft. It may be fat. Maybe it will look the same as it did before.

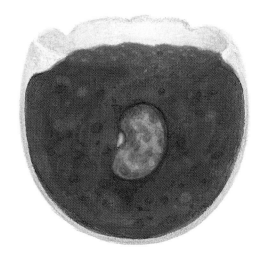

Soon the seed will grow so fat that its skin will pop off.

In two more days dig up seed Number 2.

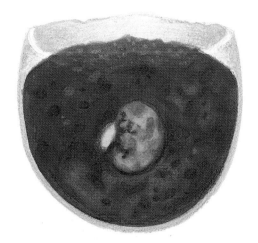

Maybe it will look different now. Maybe the skin of this seed will be loose.

Now a root starts to grow. The root grows from one side of the bean seed.

The root pushes down into the soil, down and down.

Dig up seed Number 3. Can you see the root? Does it look like this?

If you do not see a root, wait for another day. Then dig up seed Number 4.

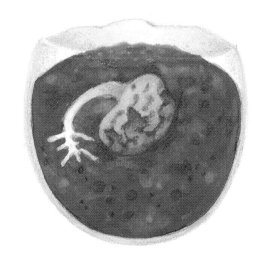

After a few more days, dig up seed Number 5. Something else is happening. Little roots will be growing from the big root. They look like tiny white hairs. They are called root hairs.

Day after day the roots and root hairs push down into the soil.

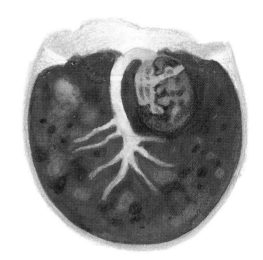

Day after day the bean seeds are pushed up. The soil is pushed aside.

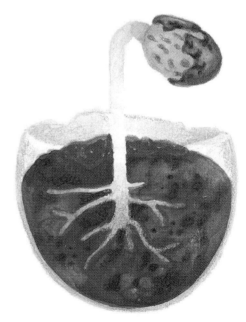

Watch your seeds. Soon you will see pale shoots push through the soil. A shoot is the beginning of a green plant. A shoot grows toward the sun.

Watch your seeds. Some may have come through the ground. Some may have broken open. Maybe some of your seeds have not started to grow.

How many are growing? Count them.

The bean seeds grow fast. The shoots turn green.

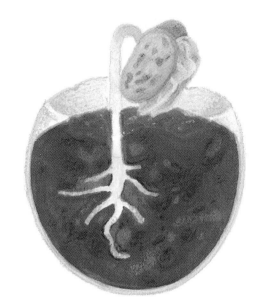

The leaves come next. Now your bean seeds are bean plants. They look like this.

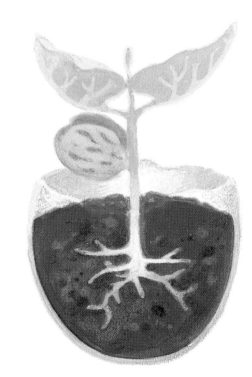

How many of your bean seeds are bean plants?

A seed needs many things to grow.

It needs soil

and water

and sun.

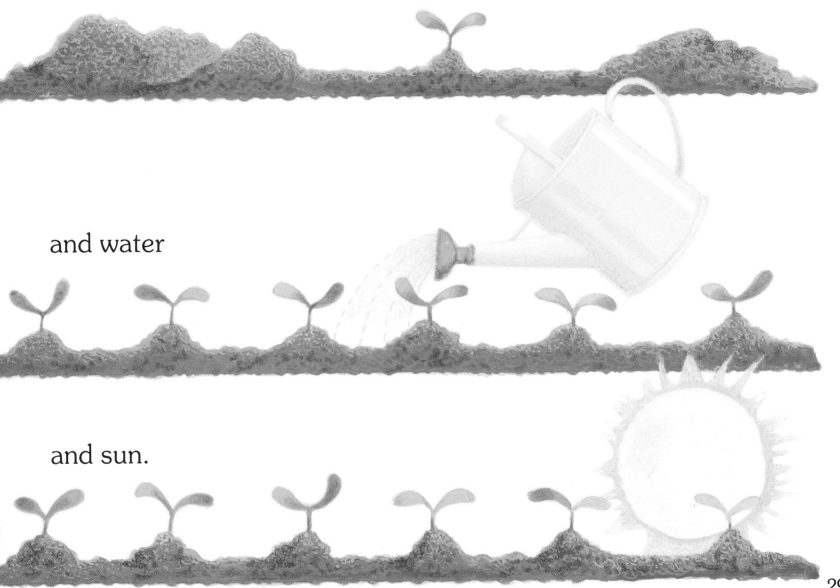

If a seed has all these things, it will grow into a plant. It will grow into the same kind of plant that it came from—an apple tree, or a daisy, or carrots, or corn. It will grow into clover or it will grow into a bean plant like the ones you planted.

FIND OUT MORE ABOUT SEEDS

Now you know that a seed needs soil, water, and sunlight to grow. Air is also important to a seed. What happens when a seed doesn't get everything it needs to grow? Or gets too much of something?

To find out, you will need:

5 plastic cups

cotton balls or tissue paper

a packet of cress seeds

1. Number the cups from 1 to 5. Fill them with cotton balls or tissue paper, and put some seeds on top in each one.
2. Put cup 1 on a windowsill with plenty of light. Sprinkle water into the cup every day for seven days.
3. Put cup 2 on the same windowsill, but do not add any water to it for seven days.
4. Put cup 3 next to cup 2. Have an adult boil some water for you. When the water is cool, pour it into cup 3 until the cup is full.
5. Put cup 4 in the refrigerator, and sprinkle water into the cup every day for seven days.
6. Put cup 5 in a dark box in a warm place, and sprinkle water into the cup every day for seven days.
7. Look at your seeds every day for seven days. What is different about the seeds in each of the cups? What are the best conditions for seeds? What are the worst?